Stories of a Dog Named Misty

by

Marjorie H. White

AuthorHouse™
1663 Liberty Drive, Suite 200
Bloomington, IN 47403
www.authorhouse.com
Phone: 1-800-839-8640

First published by AuthorHouse 9/5/2008

ISBN: 978-1-4343-8406-5 (sc)

Printed in the United States of America
Bloomington, Indiana

This book is printed on acid-free paper.

authorHOUSE®

CHAPTER I
Misty—the Very Beginning

I am a Cairn terrier and I was born—I don't remember where. I do know that I ended up on a farm, with one brother and one sister. We used to play and roll in the grass and have a great time together. However, one day this man and woman came to see us, and next thing I knew, I was in a car, driving away. This was a totally new experience for me, and I can't say I didn't like it. I would have liked it better if my brother and sister were with me.

The couple was very nice to me, and they stroked me and cooed to me, because I really was very little—and if I do say so myself—very cute. After all, I was only eight weeks old.

They took me to a house in Sutton, Massachusetts, and I started running around like crazy. In that house, you could run in one big circle, but—oops! Next thing I knew, I was rolling down some stairs. But I didn't get hurt. But the couple was very worried about me. It seemed all the dogs they had in the past were really big ones, and they weren't used to half-pints like me.

When it was time to go to bed, they put me into a cage and I cried all night. Then, in the morning, they gave me breakfast and I curled up on the comfortable rug and went to sleep. But they were kind of grouchy that day; I didn't know why—after all, they were in bed all night.

I became quite used to my new home, and everyone was good to me. I kept crying for several nights until I was invited into the bed to sleep—it was great! It was soft, nice, and cozy warm. I wrapped myself around my master's head—he didn't seem to like that, but eventually he got used to it.

One day, two weeks later (when I was ten weeks old) I was on the deck with my male person and two other friends of his. We were cooking on the barbecue grill, and it did smell very good, but I never got food that smelled that good. While they were talking and having a good time drinking some brown liquid, I was investigating, and went under the railing. Next thing I knew, I was falling through the air and landed with a real thump on the ground, about five feet lower than everyone else. They heard me land with an "oomph" coming out of my mouth. My master told everyone "Don't tell Marge." (She is my mistress and gets mad when they don't pay any attention to what I am doing.) She must think I am going to get into some mischief. I, of course, wouldn't even think of such a thing. Anyway, as it turns out, I was fine—no broken bones or telltale signs of injury.

One day, that first summer of my life, my—let's start calling the couple who adopted me *Mom* and *Dad*—mom opened the back door on the deck and said something to my dad—what an opportunity! I pushed by her, and down the stairs I went. (They didn't know I could handle stairs yet.) I flew out into the yard with Mom and Dad both chasing me. I went through a hole in the wall and went next door to visit my neighbors—Bill and Carly. Carly was a little girl, and she liked running around the yard with me when I was on a leash. And she was the one who finally caught me because I went to her. I like little girls and boys.

I was now growing up, and winter was on its way. They had to dig a path for me to go to the bathroom, because I would have been buried in the snow. I didn't like the snow—it was cold—but it was kind of fun to run in. We had a pile of turkeys who used to come by. Where they had walked, it was fun to roll in the snow and get the nice smell of turkeys all of over me. That meant, of course, that I had to have a bath before I could go into the house. I don't care for baths—I'd rather smell.

One day, when I was seven-and-a-half months old, a big green tree and several boxes full of stuff showed up in the living room. I soon found out that this was the beginning of Christmas. I got into a little trouble that day, putting my nose into places where it wasn't supposed to be—but it was a lot of fun. My mom decorated the tree with little bulbs and balls and silver shiny ropes—and everybody was so worried that I was going to do some chewing. But I couldn't chew any wires or do anything to spoil the tree because that night, when my mom lit it, everything looked so beautiful.

I found out that the next day—Christmas Day—was very special too. First, my mom dressed me up with a little red and white hat and coat. There were presents and every-thing—I got a grey bunny rabbit that squeaked; it was very long and lots of fun to play with. I got a big carrot that squeaked also, and a rubber drumstick. I sure will look forward to next Christmas.

Spring finally came in all its glory—sunshine and warm weather; this seemed to take all that snow away. The flowers were beautiful and there were leaves on the trees. Butterflies fluttered by and the birds sang. I liked this time of year. And then the best day happened! On May 13, I was one year old and I was finally a big girl. I got birthday cards and toys—a football and a squeaking pineapple. I loved it—it's too bad these things don't happen every day.

Well, that's the high times in the first year of my life. I will continue this in another short story—watch for it.

X mas
2003

CHAPTER II
The Story of Misty and Patches

I am a Cairn terrier, and I come from a long line of terriers, a mix of Scottie dog and wolf and one other dog that I can't remember. I am quite small and tan—Cairns can be black, tan, red, or brindle (which is a combination of colors). We are very peppy dogs—full of life and spirit. We are absolute imps. I am all of these things.

I like to look out of windows and bark at everything that moves—people, squirrels, chipmunks, mice, and above all—cats. I once had a friend named Patches—a black and white cat who belonged to Carly, the little girl next door. When Patches walked through the front yard, and I was lying in my usual spot in the sun in the picture window, I would have to make a whole lot of noise, barking at him and running around the house like a crazy dog.

The dog that lived here before me was a yellow Lab named Max, and he was very good friends with Patches. Patches could come into the house, walk through all the rooms, and sniff Max, who was usually sleeping (and paying no attention at all to Patches). In fact, he was quite welcome until I came to live here.

One day, when I was lying in the window, my mom fed Patches, and he came into our house. Well, we had a regular free-for-all. I put the hair up on my back to let everyone know that I didn't like him in my house. Actually, we were about the same size. I had a great time chasing the cat over tables, through bedrooms, the den, the living room, and finally down the stairs into the cellar! My dad finally opened the garage door and let Patches out while my mom held me back. I was very naughty, but it was fun.

Another time, when my mom was walking me out in the back yard, I saw Patches laying on the stone wall. I took off so fast that the leash slipped from my mom's hand. The cat and I were running wild in the woods until Patches finally went up a tree, and I had to stay on the ground, barking. The cat was in the tree for two days until his owner finally got a ladder and went up to get him. Imagine, Patches hadn't eaten or drunk anything for two days. All I got was a bunch of ticks in my fur and a scolding from my mom.

Another incident between the two of us ended up quite dangerously. I'm sure you know that kids just don't walk in the middle of the road. Well, animals shouldn't either, but sometimes they do.

This particular day, my mom was doing some house cleaning. She opened the back door to shake a rug and, lo and behold, Patches was outside on the step. Well, I bolted out of the door, practically knocking Mom on the floor—and the race began. This time, Patches didn't go up a tree; he went straight to the road in front of our house, with me about six feet behind him. And we ran straight down the middle of the road—traffic was watching us and not daring to move their cars. This was really a scary thing for my mom. Finally, I decided to stop and see my neighbor, Steve, who was cooking hot dogs for his company. Well, my mom and now my dad were still after me, but I wouldn't go to them. But finally, John—my other neighbor—grabbed me by the collar and my mom clicked the leash onto me. It was a pretty fun time. I don't know what happened to Patches—I guess he just went home, but I got a hot dog out of it, so it was worth all the scolding.

I have so many toys—every birthday and Christmas, I get three or four new toys, and while I always pull the squeaker out of them, I never destroy them. I know each and every one by name—there's Boney, Baby, Fuzzy, Shoe, Piney, Pully, Ball (and lots of others I can't even remember the names of). Some I don't play with for months at a time, but I remember the name of a long-lost friendly toy, and if my mom says, "Misty, where's Skinny?" I'll go and get Skinny. I hate to admit it, but I am very smart.

A very sad thing happened to me this year. All of a sudden, my dad—who took me for so many rides in his truck—seemed to be sick; I don't know what was wrong. But I missed our rides and all the walks he used to take me on into the woods and fields. He sometimes took me fishing too. I lay on the couch with him a lot of the time, trying to make him feel better.

My uncle Donny and cousin Donny started coming to the house a lot. They cleaned out the attic and cellar and shed. They made some fun times for me, but things were just different. Then, one Sunday morning, a truck with a siren on top of it came and took my dad away. My mom went too and my neighbor John took care of me for a while. I never saw my dad again.

My mom and I lived together, and she seemed pretty sad too. My uncle Donny and cousin Donny still kept coming every weekend to mow the lawn and do all that stuff my dad used to do.

Well, I'm going to close this episode now. I'll see you soon, in the story about me moving into a new house. See you then!

CHAPTER III
Misty and Her New House

One day, a big truck came to the house and took everything away. I didn't know what was happening—I was across the street in John's house, watching what was happening. I didn't know what was going on until my mom came to get me that evening. She took me off in the car, and we ended up at a new condo.

It was a very big mansion, and other people lived in the house also. But the best thing about the house was that I could lie on the back of the couch and see all up and down the street and watch the squirrels, chipmunks, cats, and birds at play—just like I used to do in my old house. Actually, there was more to watch in the new house, because there were a lot of people and cars too.

When my mom walked me, people would come out of their houses to say hi and introduce themselves. They made a big fuss over me. I met lots of people, and I liked the attention.

First, there was Janet and Dave next door—they were lots of fun, and my mom and I would sit on their front patio with them at night in the summer. They have three grand-daughters—Sam, Krissy, and Becky. Becky is little, and she runs out to greet me every time I go out of the house. We have a lot of fun together. And Krissy draws me doghouses with chalk on the driveway.

Then I met Shirley—she gave me lots of toys, and I had a really good time playing with Dancer, Ruby, and especially Pinky (all toys). She always comes to greet me when I am out on my walks.

I like Pam a lot too. She comes home from work in the morning, just as I am going out for my morning walk, and she gives me treats. She also feeds the squirrels, cats, and birds. She loves all of them. She is a very nice lady.

I also look for Miles—a tiger-like cat—who is owned by Elaine. Elaine likes to pet me. One Sunday on my evening walk, we saw Miles walk into an open garage, then we didn't see him for days. Finally, my mom told Elaine about seeing him go into the garage, so Elaine went across the street to the garage, and the man who owned it let her in. Lo and behold, there was Miles, meowing at the top of his lungs. Elaine was very grateful to us for having seen Miles walk into the garage. Miles is Elaine's only live-in companion, as I am my mom's.

One day, another woman moved in upstairs. She had three dogs and four cats. My mom started being careful when she took me for my walks, so that we didn't meet up in the hallways. But when she takes them out and I know that they are there, I have a great time barking at them. I make sure I am safe in my condo, though, because they are very big dogs.

There does seem to be a problem with my new house. It seems that I have developed an allergy. While I haven't been tested to see what it is, they think it is probably either pollen (which is what makes flowers and grass grow) or mold (which is that green stuff all over everything). I have to take lots of Benadryl to stop my itching.

I take it three times a day, and my mom has to wash and powder my feet every time I go out. I don't complain too much, but I don't like doing this at all—it's a pain! I even had to go to the doctor several times this summer. It's winter now, and I am much better, but I hope it doesn't come back next summer. It makes my paws itchy, and I chew them all the time—I made an infection in one paw once because I chewed and licked it.

Now that it's winter, there aren't many places to walk, so our go-out times are very short. It is okay if the snow is soft and not very deep; I can run and roll in it. But sometimes it is very hard, and that is okay too, because I can walk on top of it, but it isn't as much fun.

However, spring was just around the corner, and with it, of course, my first birthday in my new house. I was four years old (and no more grown up than on my first birthday). As usual, I had a great time opening my presents, which were a turkey leg and a fuzzy toy I named "Fuzzy," and some new treats. (I like treats.) However, I like the toys best, because they squeak and it's fun to make noise.

There was just one thing I didn't like about my new house. My uncle and cousin Donny don't come by as much as they used to. I guess there isn't as much work to do. They come on Saturdays occasionally, and we have fun when they do. I like seeing them.

Also, I don't get to see John and Steve as much, but they come by to visit us now and then. My mom takes me back to Sutton to visit them also.

Well, now that I'm used to my new house, we'll close this story and you can look forward to a new one in the very near future.

CHAPTER IV
Misty and Friends

I have many friends who have been very good to me.

However, my very best friend so far has been John. After my dad went away, he used to come over to my house and take me for long walks in the woods and the fields. I used to be on a very long leash so that I could run and run and run—I just loved it. In my new house, John still comes to visit because he helps my mom with her computer. Sometimes, when my mom goes away, I stay at John's house and we visit Steve and run in the fields and the woods. It's a lot of fun.

I like to visit Steve—he has a chair with a lot of stuffed animals in it, and I go and visit with them in their chair.

Every now and then, my mom takes me to Rhode Island to visit my aunt Margie. That's a long ride in the car. Sometimes, my mom leaves me with her and goes to visit her girl-friends. My mom came from Rhode Island. When we are at her house, my mom sleeps on the couch, and that doesn't leave me much room for sleeping, so I leave her and go into my aunt's bedroom and join her in her bed. She gets a big kick out of it. However, my mom always tells me in the morning, "You traitor, you!

At my new house, I also have many friends.

There's Janet and Dave. Dave is very good to me—he strokes me and talks to me all the time. Janet always comes out to see me and she brings Becky. Becky is a little girl about my age—four years old. She likes to see me. Becky is Janet's granddaughter. There is Krissy and Sam also. They stay with their grandmother while their mother is working. In the morning, Janet will sometimes come out to get me and take me into the house. I love running around in there—there are a lot of new smells and I have a great time.

Also, there is Pam, who gives me all kinds of treats when I am out for a walk—she is a very nice lady. And then there is Shirley, who gives me toys when I'm out for walks. Elaine is very nice to me too. She has a cat (Miles, who I have talked about previously). Once, Pam gave me two shirts to wear for Halloween—they fit me well. She used to have a dog like me—only it was white and called a Westie.

I have another friend, Audrey, who visits now and then. She stays for lunch sometimes. Her husband, Bruce, comes to visit us for our annual Christmas party. Once, on a Sunday, I went to Audrey's house by the lake—it was very pretty. But I don't think I behaved too well, because my mom never took me up there again.

Then, of course, there is my uncle Donny and cousin Donny—the two Donnys. At our old house, they used to come and spend every Saturday with us. They would work around the house—mowing, trimming, washing, and all that sort of stuff. They started doing this when my dad was sick. They kept it up for a long time. My cousin Donny used to stay overnight with me when my mom went on a trip. They helped my mom move into our new house. Even now, they come to visit. I really look forward to those times.

I also have a friend named Cricket. She is a dog just like me, but a slightly different color. She is one and a half months older than me, and belongs to a lady named Ann. I don't think Cricket likes me too well, because when we were still puppies, our moms put us together and Cricket tried to attack me—they haven't put us together since. But we still exchange Christmas presents.

My dad's family comes to visit us too. I love people to come to the house—I run around and bark when the doorbell rings, and then they come in and I jump all over them. My mom gets mad at me for this and tries to tell me not to, but I don't like to listen to that kind of talk. There's my aunt Gale, too, and lots of cousins, aunts, and uncles.

So, as you can see, I have a lot of friends and I hope to make more in the future.

CHAPTER V
Christmas in Misty's House

I LOVE Christmas! It's a lot of fun for a month or so—there's all kinds of things to keep me busy.

My mom starts shopping for me in November. She hangs my gifts in the cleaning closet in bags, but I know they are there. When she opens the door to that closet, I make a mad dash to see what she is going to bring out, but it's never one of my new toys. I can smell them—I know they are mine and she squeaks them through the bags once in a while, just to tease me.

Each season, my uncle Donny and my cousin Donny come by one special day. They will take all the Christmas stuff out of the cellar and put up the big tree in the corner of my living room. It's fun smelling all that stuff. (If you have been reading my stories, you can tell that I love to smell things!) They put silver and glittery balls on the tree, and then put silver tinsel around it and an angel on top. When they finally put the lights on, the tree actually shimmers and looks beautiful.

Then we put up a second tree in the den, where my mom and I play. She likes to see the tree at night when we are in the den—that is the reason for the second tree. And it usually looks beautiful too.

My mom has a big party in December, which we get ready for months ahead. There are about twenty people who come. I love running around when they arrive. My mom runs around yelling, "Don't let Misty out!" She's so afraid I am going to get out of the house loose. (I'll tell you a secret—there's too much going on for me to want to get out loose—I'd rather stay in this night, but don't tell my mom.)

It's so much fun when everyone is arriving, but afterward, it gets boring because no one pays attention to me after the party has begun. Once in a while, I get a tidbit, but that's all. I generally exit to go under the bed for a nap until it's time to eat. When my mom says it's time to eat, I come out and go into the kitchen where everyone is with the food, to see what I can get. It is a buffet, and they have party poppers and hats and little toys—they seem to have a lot of fun. And everyone is talking to each other at once, so the place is really quite noisy.

After the clean-up from supper is over, we all retreat back to the living room for the best part of the evening. They all play a game with playing cards and guess what? PRESENTS! I LOVE PRESENTS! My mom pours wrapped presents out of a bag and into the middle of the floor, and if she forgets to ask my uncle Donny to hold me, I jump into the middle of the presents to unwrap them—I LOVE IT!

After the game, everyone talks and then goes home. It is a really lot of fun, and then we start getting ready for next year's party.

The next fun time at Christmas is Christmas Eve. My mom goes out and leaves me all alone, but I don't mind it. I just think about tomorrow and opening all my presents. When my mom comes home on Christmas Eve, she goes to the cleaning closet and gets out one present and lets me open it. It usually is a squeak toy.

Then, on Christmas morning, she puts all my wrapped toys in a pile on the living room floor in front of the Christmas tree, and I have a ball opening them—running from one package to the next. It is the most fun time of the year. Santa Claus is very good to me.

If you ever see pictures of my Christmas tree, you will note that there is a gate in front of it. That's not so I can't touch the Christmas tree; it's to stop me from going under the tree, taking out presents for everybody else, and opening them. I love to open presents and put my head into bags.

This is going to be my last story for a while, so goodbye for now, and you can watch for more stories when I can find the time to write them. I lead a very busy life, you know.

Printed in the United States
125425LV00001B